MARRIAGES THAT WORK

Imperfect copy; sell at reduced rate.

MARRIAGES THAT WORK

A. Don Augsburger
Editor

HERALD PRESS
Scottdale, Pennsylvania
Kitchener, Ontario
1984

Library of Congress Cataloging in Publication Data

Main entry under title:

Marriages that work.

   Contents: Blueprint for a strong marriage / Evelyn M. Duvall —
Sorting out marital roles / Sylvanus M. Duvall — Individuality,
freedom, and affirmation / Cecil H. Osborne — [etc.]

   1. Marriage—Religious aspects—Christianity—Addresses, essays,
lectures. 2. Marriage counselors—United States—Biography—
Addresses, essays, lectures.
I. Augsburger, A. Don.
BV835.M24   1984   248.8'4   84-15637
ISBN 0-8361-3374-9

MARRIAGES THAT WORK
Copyright © 1984 by Herald Press, Scottdale, Pa. 15683
   Published simultaneously in Canada by Herald Press,
   Kitchener, Ont. N2G 4M5. All rights reserved.
Library of Congress Catalog Card Number: 84-15637
International Standard Book Number: 0-8361-3374-9
Printed in the United States of America
Design by Alice B. Shetler

90 89 88 87 86 85 84   10 9 8 7 6 5 4 3 2 1

This book is prayerfully dedicated to
the many families who shall
benefit from its pages.

Contents

Editor's Preface

1. Blueprint for a Strong Marriage
   Evelyn M. Duvall 11
2. Sorting Out Marital Roles
   Sylvanus M. Duvall 19
3. Individuality, Freedom, and Affirmation
   Cecil H. Osborne 25
4. Ninety Percent Good After Forty-Four Years
   Charlie and Martha Shedd 37
5. Marriage, Built on Covenant
   Richard C. and Doris Halverson 47
6. Marriage Must Not Be Left to Chance
   John M. and Betty Drescher 55
7. The Spiritual Foundations of Marital Success
   Paul Tournier 65
8. Marriage, a Lifelong Discovery
   William E. and Lucy Hulme 75
9. Commitment, Communication, and Creativity
   David and Vera Mace 87
10. Making a Good Marriage Better
    A. Don and Martha Augsburger 95
11. Summary and Proposed Direction
    A. Don Augsburger 103

Editor's Preface

Many marriages are in trouble. The divorce rate is distressingly high. Dozens of books and other printed helps offer advice. Marriage enrichment clinics are springing up in many areas. Family counselors and counseling centers are heavily scheduled. Yet marital problems still abound. What is the solution?

In recent years, I have become aware of the proliferation of remedial materials intended to help ailing relationships. But I have found little that is written from a preventative stance.

Marriages That Work brings together useful examples of successful coping with marriage problems and seasoned advice on how to maintain a stable lifelong marriage relationship. These helpful ideas come not only from the writers but from thirty-eight additional couples who responded candidly to a questionnaire sent to them.

You may have expected the persons selected to have successful marriages. However, professional people (even marriage counselors) are as vulnerable to marital problems as others.

The following pages offer tested insights and advice to help you improve and maintain your marriage.

If even a few couples learn how to keep molehills of tension from becoming mountains of stress, the purpose of this book will be achieved.

—A. Don Augsburger
Harrisonburg, Virginia

Blueprint for a Strong Marriage

Evelyn M. Duvall

"Love grows as it is shared, warming our lives personally and as a couple."

Evelyn is the founding director for the Association for Family Living, former executive director of the National Council of Family Relations, and author of more than 30 books on love, marriage, and family life.

BLUEPRINT FOR A STRONG MARRIAGE
Evelyn M. Duvall

Sylvanus M. Duvall was a college girl's ideal. Handsome in his new Burberry, swinging a cane he'd bought in London to celebrate his newly won Ph.D., he made a sensation when he called for me through our whirlwind courtship on campus. His approach was a new one. Instead of the compliments I heard from my other dates, he assured me I had "no glaring deficiencies." (He found plenty later on!) Like my father in one respect, he was easy-going, but hard to please. I have no recollection of either of them ever praising me. When I knocked myself out to please or impress my lover and husband, all I used to get was a quiet, "You did what I expected of you."

I remember sitting up in bed after a miscarriage, in our drafty Vermont parsonage, opening the mail to find a check for an article I had written for *The Christian Home*. My husband's response was, "Fine, I'll buy meat for Sunday dinner." That was in 1932 when we four—there were two daughters by then—survived on vegetables I'd raised in the backyard garden, macaroni and cheese, and an occasional chicken a generous neighbor brought us. So, when I was paid for an article I had written, or some Sunday school materials had been accepted, we splurged on "real meat" as Jean, our three-year-old, would exclaim. I satisfied more than one basic hunger with my writing and meetings with nearby parents, youth, and church groups in those days.

By the time we arrived in Chicago, invitations came in from farther afield. One time I was scheduled to leave on the midnight train for Washington, immediately following a faculty party we were giving in our home. I had packed my bags and briefcase and tucked them into my closet for a fast departure as soon as the last guest left. One dear soul, looking for the bathroom door, opened my closet, saw the packed bags, and had to know who was going, where and when. I confessed I was due at the White House Conference on Children the next day, and that I was leaving that night.

"But who will take care of your children?" she wondered. My husband with a warm grin I'll remember the rest of my life replied in his quiet voice, "Fortunately, our children have *two* parents." That precious memory sustained me over many of the rough spots that were still to come in our marriage.

"What'll we have for dinner?" was all too often my greeting as I would return home from an exhausting youth conference or other professional engagement across the country. I poured myself into these assignments, made the long trip home dead tired, only to find the house dirty, the girls eager for my undivided attention, and a husband who retreated behind the closed bathroom door to talk to himself just loud enough for me to hear how neglected he felt. It was almost more than I could take. For I was love-hungry too, as I realized more fully when I came to terms with my own feelings and motivation.

My father had been convinced that a university education was wasted on a woman, "She'll only get married anyway," he'd say. As an only son he had dropped out of school to work in the family business. His sister, far less able than he, graduated from the local normal school and promptly married. He rigorously opposed my going away to college when my time came, and cut me off without a penny because I was so "stubborn" about going in the face of his opposition.

My mother, on the other hand, backed my going to Syracuse University. She assured me, "You can do anything you really want to, Evelyn." She made all my clothes while scrimping on her own, and took in local college girls for meals while doing all her own cooking and baking. I can still taste her warm cherry pie and smell the hot cinnamon buns fresh from the oven on a Saturday morning. Her mother had died when she was fourteen, and her father traveled widely as a professional musician. She needed a confidante, and I as her eldest, filled that role.

With my pastor's help, Mother and I circumvented my father's opposition, got me into the university, and backed me through the three-and-a-half years to my bachelor's degree, summa cum laude. I think she was pleased, but she did not come to my graduation, because it would have infuriated my father. So my triumphal march across the platform was witnessed only by my college friends, and my future mother-in-law, who "stood-in" for her son, already in his first teaching position.

After we married and I went with Sylvanus to live in Nashville, Tennessee, that precious man of mine backed me as I enrolled in Vanderbilt University for my master's degree, and then all the way through to my Ph.D. from the University of Chicago eighteen years, two babies, and a professional career later. That dear husband of mine made my research work a family project. He'd work with the girls clearing away the supper dishes so that I could get back to my research data spread all over the dining room table. When I finally emerged from the University of Chicago chapel with my Ph.D. in my hands, our younger daughter, Joy, ran up to me, gave me a hug, and asked, "Good! That's done. Now what will we do?" The answer was *plenty*, and it wasn't easy.

Strange that the years of struggle were the easiest in our marriage. Then as things began to break for me with books published, university posts opening up, and finances no longer such a problem, the strains on our marriage peaked. My husband's job was uninspiring drudgery. We both knew it, but nothing more promising opened up for him. Together as a team we led national conferences and summer teaching posts, but there was never any question in his mind to which of us the invitation came. We both enjoyed going around the world leading family life conferences. He gloried in our assignments through the Caribbean, and for the New Zealand government later on, but even then I felt at times that he reluctantly tagged along behind.

Our worst conflicts came in the use of the money I earned from my writing and lecturing. I wanted to set up trust funds for our missionary daughter and her four sons, with custodial accounts for our grandchildren's education, so that they would not have to struggle as we had. But my husband rarely gave gifts to anyone, insisting that being generous only weakened the recipient's ability to fend for himself or herself. We argued and could not see eye to eye on the issue. We finally worked through our money matters by making me the family accountant, in charge of computing our joint taxes, paying our bills, and most importantly investing funds for our future security with little thought of the original source of the funds.

We have come to realize that we are two basically different persons trying to get through to one another across the gulf of our differences. He is something of a recluse, happiest behind closed doors with his books, his typewriter, and his thoughts. I am a "people-person" delighting in my relationships with others individually and in groups. He is a thinker; I am a doer. He is quiet, often monosyllabic; I tend to talk too much. He and I are as different as can be. It is a miracle that we have learned to live with our differences so comfortably.

As each of us came to accept the dynamics of our own drives, I relaxed and began to appreciate my husband for the fine man he is, with keen social and intellectual interests, decades of encouraging me to be a person in my own right, and a growing ability to express his love for me. One evidence of this is his willingness now to share his feelings with me face to face, rather than talk them out to himself—a practice that always bothered me. For my part, I have learned to respect his need for privacy. I go about the business of caring for his creature comforts without disturbing his train of thought with mundane matters. We now have established a comfortable daily routine that brings us satisfaction greater than either of us has known before.

How did we do it? Not by "solving" all our problems, but rather by recognizing that:

1. Problems are a part of marriage as they are of life itself.

2. Both of us are fine persons with assets and liabilities that are our total "personality package."

3. Open discussion and airing of our real feelings are mutually helpful.

4. Love grows as it is shared, warming our lives personally and as a couple.

Now in retirement in an idyllic setting in a community of congenial friends and neighbors, we are at peace with ourselves, with one another, and with the world at large. We have grown individually and as a couple to the place where we are happy in our service-oriented daughters, our fine grandchildren and great-grandchildren. We are comfortable not only in a physical sense, but more deeply as persons who have discovered who we are, as well as what we can be and do.

More than ever before we are deeply in love with life and with one another.

Sorting Out Marital Roles

Sylvanus Milne Duvall

"I have experienced what love can mean."

Sylvanus taught religion and social science for forty years. Since retirement in 1966 he has sought, mainly through history and social psychology, better answers to such questions as:
—What turns people on?
—Why do highly educated people often make such stupid blunders?
—How can our increasing knowledge become wisdom?
—How can religious faith become more valid, vital, and beneficial?
The findings, although still meager, have been exciting.

SORTING OUT MARITAL ROLES
Sylvanus M. Duvall

The morning has been routine. Breakfast is over and the dishes washed. My wife has just left for an appointment, while I have settled down to review more than 54 years of marriage. It is not easy, this sharing of personal intimacies with the public. We are both human beings with many faults and foibles. Human beings rarely have idyllic relationships in marriage or in anything else. We have won, though, and because this has not been easy, our story may be helpful to others.

The first serious conflict to affect our family was not with each other, but with our bishop. We were married in December 1927, during my second year as professor of religious education at Scarritt College, Nashville. I was thoroughly committed to Christ who made serious demands upon me regarding social issues. The bishop was also committed to Christ; but his Christ and mine did not agree.

In 1931 I was out of a job in the depth of the Depression. I held small pastorates for the next three years, when our economic strains were severe. Then, taking advantage of graduate study at the London School of

Economics, I went to George Williams College as professor of social science and religion. We remained in Chicago for 32 years. While there, my wife became established in her career, out of which major conflicts and adjustments arose in our marriage.

During the first ten years of marriage we had no severe marital conflicts. In all our difficulties, financial and otherwise, my wife stood loyally by me at every turn. Our first year in Chicago, the local Child Study Association employed Mrs. Duvall to lead parent groups. This caused no problems in our family. Then, because of her unusual success, she became executive of a reorganized association, and our career conflicts began.

I knew at the time of our marriage that she was a person of unusual ability. Her scientific research as a student had been of considerable commercial importance. She earned her master's degree at Vanderbilt while carrying our first child. I expected that as soon as our children were grown, she would have a career. I did not realize that she was as able as she proved to be, nor that when she took on a task, she had to give it all she had.

When she became executive director of the Association for Family Living, both of these qualities emerged. The organization boomed. It also absorbed more and more of her energy and time. She continued to attend events at my college and to entertain faculty and students, but these were not her chief interests. Meanwhile, I was expected to attend numerous affairs important to the public relations of her community activities. We also had a household with two children for whom I took increasing responsibility, around the edges of a series of "housekeepers" who were hard to find and keep through the war years.

Vocationally, my wife became increasingly successful. From the local agency she went on to become executive director of the National Council on Family Relations. This too flourished. In the meantime, she had completed her Ph.D., had written several books, and was giving hundreds of lectures a year, some to important national assemblies. From these she would return home utterly spent. No doubt about it, she needed a full-time "wife."

This role I neither would nor could assume. Since I am somewhat lazy and easygoing, her success did not bother my "male ego." But I was not willing to sacrifice my career nor my own identity. I enjoyed looking after the children, and as they became older they took on much of the routine housework. I resisted and resented being forced to neglect my work at the college and to curtail activities that were important to me. These conflicts were both rough and deep. One church leader who often involved Mrs. Duvall in his programs, told me privately that he was surprised that we had remained married to each other. Here are some reasons why we could and did.

First, we were essentially sound persons. Neuroses are as common as cavities in the teeth, and we both had plenty of them. But we were able to handle them. There were no sexual digressions. Despite the strength of her emotional drives, my wife is essentially sound. When the chips were down, she always came through.

Second, we both wanted our marriage to succeed. It wasn't easy. Each of us had to take a lot from the other. We came through because we were willing to work hard to succeed.

Third, we each had a considerable knowledge of human behavior. This helped us to understand and accept both ourselves and each other.

Fourth, we were and are growing persons. Personally, I was helped by an increasing awareness of my own limitations. Increased knowledge resulted in greater wisdom, including the recognition that I was a normal "nice guy" but somewhat mediocre. My wife was the much abler person. This was a matter of regret, but not of shame. Good mental health has given me an edge on those who are much smarter than I. I came to see that my wife's career was more important than mine. I was not willing to become absorbed. I was willing to subordinate my career to hers, and to give support without resentment. I was growing up.

This realism has transformed our married life. As my wife also matured, her compulsions diminished. She emerged in all her loveliness and beauty. I recognized how fortunate I was to be her husband. It was then that love reached its fulfillment and its joy. After 54 years of marriage I thrill to hear her key in the lock and rejoice in her cheery greeting. Although the fires of youth have dampened considerably, holding her in my arms is sheer joy. I note with gratitude the many signs of her love for me. I see how often she overlooks my foibles in a love that is more than forgiveness. Conflicts still take place, often sharp. They are now overwhelmed in a love that "passeth understanding."

This working through of our marriage gives me hope for mankind. I have experienced what love can mean. If the Duvalls can work through the brambles and stupidities of their neuroses, so can others. So, perhaps, can nations. Therefore, we have hope for our children, our grandchildren, and our great-grandchildren, of whom we have two.

We rejoice in God, and in each other.

Individuality, Freedom, and Affirmation

Cecil H. Osborne

"*Every marriage experiences tensions. It is impossible to live in the same house with another person in such a close relationship without problems arising.*"

Cecil is the founder-director of Yokefellows, Inc., and the Burlingame Counseling Center. He pioneered in the discovery and development of Primal Integration therapy.

He has written ten books; the latest is *The Joy of Understanding Your Faith*.

INDIVIDUALITY, FREEDOM, AND AFFIRMATION
Cecil G. Osborne

I was seventeen years old, and very much in love. At the time I was not aware of the truism that "puppy love can lead to a dog's life," but I do recall a wild mixture of emotions when I proposed to the young woman with whom I lived for 56 years. I was about to make a lifetime commitment.

The night before I decided to propose to her, I prayed earnestly for divine guidance. I most certainly did not want to make a mistake.

Ours was a thoroughly successful marriage relationship because of a number of factors. We both had the same general religious background, although mine was much more legalistic than hers. We each earnestly sought the will of God in our lives. Although we felt physically, emotionally, and spiritually attracted to each other, we sensed that other elements are also essential to a happy marriage. Communication is one of the most important of these. There have probably been more books written on marriage in the past six months than were published in the 50 years before we were married.

Our marriage took place while I was still in school, with

two more years of seminary work before me. I often said to my wife who died not so long ago that she had one fault which I hoped she would correct. "You don't complain enough," I said to her. It was a half facetious comment, but what I meant was that she never complained enough to let me know even when she was unhappy. We spent the first two years in a tiny one-room apartment with a kitchenette with walls you could touch by standing in the middle of the room. She never complained, but she was not a martyr.

Early in the marriage we experienced some of the standard conflicts which afflict most young couples. However, these were minor. Though my wife was not a critical person, there was much in me and my conduct to criticize; but there was a marvelous tolerance and understanding in her attitude.

It was only years later that I came to realize that no one person can satisfy all of our needs. There had been some of the normal tensions in our relationship. It became apparent to me one day that I had no right to expect her to meet all of my mental, physical, spiritual, emotional, and domestic needs. No one can give unconditional love all the time. And yet all of us consciously or unconsciously expect it, or at least need it. I think the revelation that we could not supply all of each other's needs was the most important insight that I ever had. At that point I stopped expecting her to be the idealized mother and wife. Some of the unrealistic expectations absorbed earlier from romantic novels, movies, and poetry gave way to the realities of everyday living.

Marriage is certainly the most difficult of all relationships, primarily because two people are thrown together and expected to relate in total harmony without serious disagreement, with common interests, goals, and aspirations, for the rest of their lives.

I once went fishing with a close friend of mine whom I had known and admired for many years. We were together for five days. After the second day I could barely stand him. There were irritating qualities in his personality which grated on me. We are still good friends, but I would never go on a vacation with him again. Living closely together as in marriage brings out the best and the worst in people. Personality traits which seemed minor irritations before taking the wedding vows, become glaring and disastrous faults in the day-to-day relationship of marriage.

Every marriage experiences tensions. It is impossible to live in the same house with another person in such a close relationship without problems arising. Misunderstandings occur. Occasionally communication breaks down.

I was not the world's best communicator. In the early days of marriage I tended to withdraw at times, finding it not only difficult to communicate when feeling angry, but absolutely impossible. It wasn't that I wouldn't talk; I *couldn't*. This rather lamentable trait was the result of having learned at the end of a big stick never to talk back to mother. Mother equalled all women. In a verbal encounter with my wife I would simply freeze emotionally.

Eventually I discovered that if I could respond within the first five or ten seconds, I could express myself. But if the response was delayed much longer, the minor resentment turned to anger and then into a kind of frozen rage. The emotion was out of all proportion to the precipitating cause. It simply meant that my innocent wife had pushed some old red button on my control panel, causing unresolved primal feelings to surface.

Eventually I learned to respond in the first few seconds, with a statement such as, "When you say things like that I feel upset." This is more of an "I" message, telling how I felt, than a "you" message, which is usually accusatory. Each of us has a right to our feelings. They are always valid. They need not be logical, but if they can be expressed in an uncritical and nonjudgmental manner, communication can take place. Whenever communication broke down it was almost invariably my fault.

Communication improved when I learned to respond in those first five or ten seconds. It also helped when my wife learned that there were certain red buttons on my control panel which she shouldn't push. I also learned which red buttons on her control panel I had to avoid.

For instance, without even discussing the issue, we resolved early in the marriage never to criticize each other's relatives. It was all right for me to offer a critical comment concerning one of mine, but for some totally illogical reason I would not have appreciated her offering the same criticism. One's relatives are an extension of one's own personality. To attack someone's father, mother, brother, sister, uncle, or aunt is nearly always perceived as an attack upon the self.

A wise reticence is essential in any successful marital relationship. Some subjects should be avoided. This is not a cop-out. This is simply the principle of treating one's husband or wife with as much courtesy and tact as would be used with some stranger whom you will never see again.

In a polite social encounter we do not criticize the opinions, religion, politics, or relatives of the person to whom we've just been introduced. We are incredibly polite and considerate. But it is not uncommon for a couple, on the way home from a social event, to engage in hostile criticism of how the other behaved during the evening. Common ordinary courtesy and tact are an absolutely essential ingredient in any successful relationship, particularly marriage.

Someone once said facetiously that there are three words which every woman loves to hear from her husband—"I was wrong." Actually it is extremely difficult for most people to utter those magical words. The weaker our self-esteem, the less self-worth we have, the harder it is to admit that we were wrong. In our 56 years of marriage my wife and I learned the wisdom and the importance of admitting freely when we were wrong, or when one of us had simply been out of focus emotionally, or unduly upset.

One of the most important decisions my wife and I ever made came about as a result of some minor conflict. I had been trying subtly to maneuver her into some action I considered desirable. No one likes to be controlled or changed. When we try to change people, we make them angry. She rather understandably had been trying to change me in certain ways. I am certain that I needed those changes. However, neither of us were succeeding. In a few minutes of discussion we arrived at one of the most important decisions that any couple could ever make. It was this:

1. We agreed that we would never try to *change* each other.

2. We agreed that we would not try to *control* each other.

3. We decided that we would never *criticize* each other, no matter what the provocation.

It seemed at first as though this had cut off a great deal

of our communication, so we added a fourth factor which was this:

4. We agreed that whenever either of us was displeased, we had the right and even the obligation to say, "I am displeased or unhappy when you do a certain thing." That comment simply sends a message, but does not demand that the other make a change.

We were both well aware of the threefold truth that, "I can change no other person by direct action; I can change only myself; and when I change, others tend to change in reaction to me."

After we made that important decision, we seemed to pull apart for a time. Then I noticed that my wife was making more of an effort to meet my needs. In response I endeavored to find out what her needs were, and tried to meet more of them. For instance, she liked to go out to dinner. We had been eating out once a week, and in an effort to make her happier, I suggested that we go out at least twice a week. At times we simply ended up at a hamburger stand. On other occasions we ate at a first-class restaurant. The important thing was that she liked to get out of the house and eat someone else's cooking.

Another discovery I made was that I had not been giving her as much verbal affirmation as she might have appreciated. She made no complaint about it, and I learned about it only by accident. Since this was a legitimate need, I set about trying to meet that need by expressing deep appreciation more frequently. This involved approval of her appearance when she dressed up, of her performance, or even of a good meal. Everyone without exception appreciates being appreciated. I confess, however, that I was not as diligent or as thoughtful in this area for a good many years as I might have been.

We humans tend to marry for one main reason: *To have our own needs met.* When the other person does not fulfill all of our multitudinous needs, we tend to become irritated or angry. We then spend an enormous amount of energy trying to manipulate the other person into a position where our needs can be met. The solution, I believe, is to try to discover the needs of the other person and endeavor to meet those needs.

Somewhere along the line it suddenly occurred to me that love is not simply an emotion, but an action. Married love must involve *agape* love also, or the marriage can flounder. Agape, or Christian love, is as concerned about the needs and the feelings of the other person as about our own. It suggests unconditional acceptance, even though the actions of another person may seem unacceptable at the time.

One of the most helpful ingredients in our marriage involved compromise. Obviously if two people want different things at the same time, they cannot both be gratified. My wife and I had made numerous trips to Europe, the Middle East, and the Far East, and eventually I decided I wanted to go to Kathmandu, the capital of Nepal. I also wanted to go to Isfahan, an ancient city in Iran.

My wife said, in a semihumorous vein, that she didn't want to go to Kathmandu and stay in a goat hair tent. I explained that there were first-class hotels even in Nepal. She asked why I wanted to go to those weird places. I explained that I liked the sound of their names, and could really give no other valid reason. She said rather quietly that she had always wanted to go back to Austria, which she loved. I had no interest in going to Austria a second time. This could have been a minor impasse. We resolved it in about thirty seconds by my saying, "All right, this year we will go to Austria, and on our next trip we will go to Kathmandu and Isfahan." She said, "Fine." I actually had a very good time in Austria, and the following year we took in the two exotic cities which I had always wanted to visit, together with some others, and she enjoyed the trip immensely.

Compromise is one of the most important keys in any human relationship. If I want to go to an Italian restaurant and my friend or wife insists on Chinese food, we have the seeds of a problem, unless some kind of compromise can be reached. Often at our counseling center I hear wives complain, "I have to make all of the decisions. My husband is very passive, and always asks me what I would like to do. Sometimes I would like for him to make plans and decisions." I asked one wife, "What would you do if he made some plans, and the evening turned out to be a total loss?" She said with some feeling, "I'd be very upset!" I suggested that she express any discontent with his choices in as tactful a way as possible. I said, "If you really want him to learn how to take the initiative more often, don't blow it by criticizing his choices."

Marriage can be the most gratifying and fulfilling of all relationships; it can also be one of the most frustrating. About 65 percent of all marriages could be improved by some type of counseling. It has been my experience that about one third of marriages are extremely happy; one third of the couples are held together by debt, children, or a sadomasochistic relationship; and another third end in divorce. Unfortunately many men feel reluctant to seek out a marriage counselor, often until it is too late. The male ego is such that the husband frequently feels reluctant to share his personal problems with a third person. A typical response is, "We're adults; we'll work this out ourselves." Often it is only after the wife has filed suit for divorce that a distraught husband will call in panic and ask what can be done to get his wife back.

I would think it would have been very helpful if some wise person had said to me just prior to our marriage, "Young man, the most important thing I want to convey to you is the knowledge that no one person can fulfill all of your needs. Do not expect it, but try to fulfill as many of your wife's needs as possible and your marriage will flourish."

Ninety Percent Good After Forty-Four Years

Charlie and Martha Shedd

"*We've been loving each other for forty-four years, and in our opinion we have the best marriage ever.*"

Charlie and Martha live on Fripp Island, South Carolina. Irrepressible, both bubble with enthusiasm for life. Their Christian faith pervades their conversation---naturally and easily, but unfailingly. One can't be around them five minutes without knowing that they believe life is God-given, and that it's unbelievably great when it's lived as God intends.

Recognized as authorities on marriage enrichment, the Shedds have authored more than 30 books, many of them bestsellers.

NINETY PERCENT GOOD AFTER FORTY-FOUR YEARS

Charlie and Martha Shedd

How do you grade your marriage today? The following test may help you decide.

We were asked to share the secrets of our love. But first we'll talk about your love. For you, your marriage is more important than ours. That's why we begin with a questionnaire.

Procedure: In your evaluation, the idea is for husband and wife to grade the relationship separately. We suggest that you approach this test alone, and after careful thought, answer each question individually. Mark your grades on a separate sheet (not on the book page) so your mate can answer without prejudice. Then sometime later (when the time, energy level, and relationship are right) compare grades, discuss, and begin closing gaps. In a recent California seminar one husband graded their marriage 97. His wife gave it a 42. That must have made for some lively sessions between them.

Good luck, think hard, have fun, and may this kind of probing do for your love what it does for us.

The Marriage Questionnaire
(Using the 1 to 100 grading system, rate the following, 70 for passing)

Overall
　　1. Compared to the hopes I had when we married, compared to most other couples I know, I grade our marriage overall ____.

Communication
　　2. Our mark for the complete sharing of inner feelings, full honesty well expressed, ability and willingness to talk, I grade our relationship ____.

The little extras
　　3. For communication of the good things: praise, compliments, appreciation, thoughtfulness, verbal affection, I deserve a grade of ____. I grade my mate ____.

Hostility
　　4. At expressing things we don't like (the big negatives and little ones), I rate my mate ____. Myself ____.

Forgiving
　　5. When it comes to mercy, grace, forgiving and forgetting, I rate my attitude ____. My mate's ____.

"Spaces in our togetherness"
　　6. These four words from an ancient prophet summarize important ingredients for marriage at its growing best. For liberty to become, for respecting uniqueness in each other, for encouraging individual growth as we grow together, our relationship rates ____.

Sex
　　7. Our ability to meet each other's physical needs, to respond with uninhibited pleasure, to enjoy fully, rates a grade of ____. The honest grade for me is ____. My mate ____.

Religion
　　8. For vital religion, theological harmony of basic concepts, for a growing sense of our oneness with divine love, our grade together is ____.°

We've been loving each other for forty-four years, and in our opinion we have the best marriage ever. For us, it's the best. But that doesn't mean it's perfect. Ninety percent of the time we can say it's super. But to tell it like it is, the other ten percent can be absolutely awful.

When does a relationship reach 100 percent? We have decided it must be somewhere over the horizon into eternity. Since the Bible tells us we are neither married nor given in marriage in heaven, how will we ever reach maximum? We have an agreement on this. Whoever goes to heaven first will ask the Lord if we can be live-in buddies forever. But until that time, we plan to keep on building from ninety percent to one hundred. After all we started with fifty-one percent and from there we've gone to ninety. That's a shade less than one percent each year.

Coming at it from this "growing" viewpoint, maximum marriage seems so far away, doesn't it? "You mean forty-four years? That sounds like forever." True, sometimes it does seem like forever. But here's another piece of news straight from two who have been there—the forty-four years are sure to pass anyway! Wouldn't it be wonderful if forty-four years from now the two lovers you know best could say, "We have the finest marriage ever, for us."

So how can we reach that goal?

For us one answer is our "covenant of gifts." Theologically "covenant" means "sacred promise," "promises

---

*This particular test is adapted from the new edition of *Talk to Me: A Warm, Frank Approach to the Ways a Woman Can Get Her Man to Communicate*. Edition II, Charlie W. Shedd (Doubleday 1983). Second editions are always a special thrill for many reasons to both author and publisher. And in this case one special thrill is the hope that many new loves may be opened to deeper communication.

between two," or "holy agreements from both directions."

Most of us would insist that when we came to the altar, we meant every word of our promises. "I do," "I will," "till death do us part." Yet for most of us the awesome aspects of our pledges gradually give way to a dangerous fade-off. In the crush of everyday living we forget the awe of what we're into. Because this was true in our lives, when it began to happen, Martha and I decided on some daily, weekly reminders—little covenants to keep the big covenant alive.

But as anyone knows, even little promises get crowded out too. Why? One answer at our house is plain selfishness. We knew from the beginning that marriage is both "give" and "take." Yet early in our days together we also learned that "take" includes the taking of good intentions too. We needed some specifics to keep us in a giving mood.

That is how our "Covenant of Gifts" came to be. We have learned that even a small promise actually grows very large over the years. How many covenants do we have? Many, and here are a few of our favorites.

1. *We pledge each other the gift of time, time together alone, time for the two of us to read each other's souls.*

"Zip, zam, and zowie do we live." Whoever said it first was right on. A home to tend, children to provide for, relatives coming, neighbors to be friendly with, church work to do, plus dad's heavy job, and in many cases now mom's also. Where in this sea of endless activity can lovers ever find time to nourish their relationship?

Answer: We will not *find* time. Time for loving must be *made*. Some things we've done right. Very right. And one of the most right for us is this sacred pledge we made early in our marriage: "At least once a week we will go from our home for getting to know each other."

Usually this is a dinner date. Not an expensive place where the meal costs as much as new drapes for the living room. A pizza, hamburger, somebody's salad bar, or when the funds were very low, a long walk, a visit in the park. Anything, any place, away from our home, away from the little people, away from the doorbell, away to the interior of our love.

2. Another little agreement with mighty implications: *Every day we will give each other some simple compliment.*

Nothing stupendous here, but then again multiplied by forty-four years, couldn't it become colossal? It could and did. Was there ever a more important word than this short phrase from 1 Corinthians, "Love rejoices not at wrong, but rejoices in the right"?

"Where have all the flowers gone?" a popular song inquires. Sad message. But we decided we would take that to heart too. We would not let the "nice" get away, and one way we'd keep it coming on strong would be our covenant of the simple compliments.

We call them our "warm fuzzies." It's a term used often by our psychologist friends and we like it. "I need a warm fuzzy...." "I haven't had my warm fuzzy today...." "I want to give you a warm fuzzy." Silly? Maybe for some, but for us this "I like you because" every day is among our rarest of gifts and a sacred covenant.

Fact is we like that one so much we've added another: "Every week we will pay each other a *new* compliment."

Back to the multiplication table now and how does that figure? Forty-four years by fifty-two weeks equals 2,288 things we like about each other. Who do we like best? The people who like us. Small wonder we are absolutely wild about each other.

3. After that, would you believe all-important item three is what we choose to call, *The gift of surfaced hostility*?

Readers of our books ask us often about our "Seven Official Rules for a Good Clean Fight." Simply put these are but the breakdown of our hostility covenant. Since even the finest of loves cannot be all violins and roses, some of the greatest blessings in our personal history have come from hammering together at the anvil of solid disagreement.

When to disagree?

Some scholars focus on Paul's admonition, "Let not the sun go down on your wrath." They interpret that to mean "Settle your quarrels before bedtime." Sounds good. But in our experience that needs some thinking through. Did Paul actually mean what these scholars say? We don't think so. Or if he did mean it, we take comfort in the fact that he probably wasn't married. Some days it takes all the strength we have just to go on breathing.

We conclude, therefore, that the full biblical meaning for negative sharing goes more like this, "We can still love even when we don't like." Theologically it is solid fact: God loves us, not because we are perfect, but because we are his. And woe to the couple who sets their standard at 100 percent right now. Yet woe also to the couple who goes on forever hiding their negatives.

A wise old sage early in our marriage advised us, "If

you don't carry out the garbage, one day your house will become a dump." Shades of the poet's wording, "It is the little rift within the lute that by and by may make the music mute."

Time and space are running out, but before we close this down, we must tell you about our two most important covenants. These are the covenant of Bible study and the covenant of prayer together. For us these are gifts supreme. We have pledged each other time for sharing together out of God's Word, and praying together daily.

In two of our forthcoming books we will deal at length with how we study the Bible and as a couple how we learned to pray. Say it again, for us these are the highest of the high roads to a heavenly marriage.

We close our chapter with this guarantee: Any couple who will develop a 44-year program based on studying God's Word together and daily prayer together will one day reach maximum in every way.

Marriage, Built on Covenant

Richard C. Halverson

"When the covenant is taken seriously, however troublesome the learning-growing process, difficulties serve to deepen intimacy and mature love."

Richard, chaplain of the United States Senate, is known as a beloved pastor, an expository preacher, a Bible teacher, lecturer, and counselor. Both he and Doris have served nobly in many aspects of Christian ministry.

MARRIAGE, BUILT ON COVENANT
Richard C. and Doris Halverson

As Doris and I reflect on our marriage of nearly forty years, its trials and troubles, and our often carnal response to them, we are overwhelmingly reminded of our inadequacy in so many situations, and of God's gracious, merciful, loving patience, and generous provision and guidance.

The fact is we didn't know "how" to handle the circumstances much of the time. We stumbled, fell, recovered, struggled, and failed often, but somehow we were led gently through to resolution and blessing. With hindsight (which someone has said is an "exact science") we realize now in our terrible inadequacy that God was faithful over and over again. We were learners who did not know "how" to succeed at marriage.

It is clear that with however much knowledge a couple begins marriage, they have much more to learn and will be learning all their lives. Much like a skier, for example, who has read all that books can teach him and has received verbal instructions. Now he's at the top of a slope and he begins to learn. He starts down, falls, tries again, falls, and so on, but as he falls he is learning something to do, something not to do. Now what he read in the books or was taught by his instructor makes more sense. His knowledge is being actualized.

When the marriage covenant is taken seriously, however troublesome the learning-growing process, difficulties serve to deepen intimacy and mature love. This has been the central reality throughout our increasingly fulfilling, yet not trouble-free relationship.

If we are not careful, "how to" instructions reduce us to consideration of strategies, techniques, and tactics, which go only so far in nurturing any kind of a relationship—least of all the marital union. In this context, 1 Corinthians 13, especially verses 4 through 8, is the finest instruction available.

> "Love is patient, love is kind. It does not envy, it does not boast, it is not proud. It is not rude, it is not self-seeking, it is not easily angered, it keeps no record of wrongs. Love does not delight in evil but rejoices with the truth. It always protects, always trusts, always hopes, always perseveres. Love never fails. But where there are prophecies, they will cease; where there are tongues, they will be stilled; where there is knowledge, it will pass away" (NIV).

Often in premarital counseling, I have wished it were possible to communicate adequately to young people beginning life together the incalculable blessings available to couples who honor their marriage covenant no matter how difficult it may seem. The word that comes nearest to identifying what I, as a husband, feel is the word security. It is a condition which is the fruit of facing difficulties and misunderstandings together, of learning to request forgiveness and of forgiving. It is the product of struggle—struggle which deepens intimacy and matures love.

How interesting and significant that the struggle which divides and alienates is also the struggle that unites and bonds a relationship. The difference between dividing and uniting is the seriousness with which the covenant is taken. For Doris and me, the covenant was simply not negotiable. Everything else was. But it was settled from the beginning that we were entering into an agreement to which God was witness and we saw it as an unconditional contract for life.

Not that we thought we were stronger or more committed than others whose marriages fail. There was much, in fact, about each of us (especially me) that weakened the possibilities of a strong and enduring relationship. But the call of God to the pastoral ministry was decisive. For the sake of Christ and the ministry to which we had been called, separation and/or divorce were simply out of the question. We had to make our marriage work.

Now with the perspective of forty years together, we can see how beneficial that constraint was for us. We see now that treating the covenant as nonnegotiable helped us through very difficult times, especially in the early years.

Early tensions in the pastorate were common to many in that situation. Though unaware of it for years, I gave church work priority over wife and children. Without realizing the implications, I justified absence from home and neglect of husbandly-fatherly duties on the grounds that I was serving Christ. Long since I have learned to distinguish between serving Christ and keeping busy at church work. It was a painful lesson and my beloved wife suffered greatly because of this. I experience shame and humiliation still when I recall a kind of pious arrogance whereby I treated requests of my family almost as a virtue.

In amazement I recall how in those early days I earnestly presented Ephesians 5:21-32 to young couples contemplating marriage. "Husbands love your wives, even as Christ also loved the church, and gave himself for it." Somehow it never occurred to me that I was showing neither unconditional nor sacrificial love for my wife, as Christ did for his church.

Today that exhortation has become for me the foundation of a marriage which honors God and blesses the family. It has become clear to me that 100 percent of the responsibility for sustaining the marriage rests with the husband. This does not excuse a wife from her responsibility or failure. She is to obey Paul's exhortation as much as her husband. But neither does her failure excuse her husband from his responsibility to love her as Christ loved the church—that is unconditionally and sacrificially.

Both Jesus and Paul repeat the first instruction to the husband recorded in the Scripture. "Therefore shall a man leave his father and his mother, and shall cleave unto his wife: and they shall be one flesh" (Genesis 2:24; Matthew 19:5; Ephesians 5:31). It is the husband who is to guard the relationship against intrusion even of his parents, and to cleave to his wife. That word "cleave" means to "be glued" to his wife—or "stick to" his wife—no matter what.

In his stinging indictment of the people of God, Malachi addresses his remarks directly, admonishing and reproving, "Because the Lord was witness to the covenant between you and the wife of your youth, to whom you have been faithless, though she is your companion and your wife by covenant . . . so take heed to yourselves, and let none be faithless to the wife of his youth. For I hate divorce, says the Lord God of Israel" (Malachi 2:14-16, RSV).

The prophet Hosea portrays God as a faithful husband despite the continual failure of his wife. Hosea demonstrates the husbandly faithfulness of Christ for his church, a faithfulness which manifests itself by unconditional, sacrificial love. Husbands are to love their wives.

The covenant, taken seriously, provides the "glue" of marriage which holds it together when circumstances or emotions work to destroy the relationship. The covenant is verbalized in the marriage vows, when in the presence of God, loved ones, and friends, a man and woman pledge to receive each other and submit to each other unconditionally for life. The will is the key to this pledge. Where there is the will to honor the covenant, the will to refuse and reject every force that would dishonor it, the will to "cleave" in spite of everything, the very circumstances which might otherwise alienate a couple will be the raw material to strengthen their bond.

Human history began with a wedding in the Garden of Eden and human history ends with a wedding feast. In the love and union of one man and one woman for life, God has given us the secret of reality and fulfillment in history.

Marriage Must Not Be Left to Chance

John M. and Betty Drescher

"We have found that anything in life which is worthwhile dare not be left to chance."

Drescher has authored twenty-seven books. He has written for more than 100 different magazines and journals.

John and Betty serve as leaders of family retreats and seminars and as speakers in renewal meetings across denominational lines.

MARRIAGE MUST NOT BE LEFT TO CHANCE
John M. and Betty Drescher

Marriage is a relationship and a relationship is a living, life-giving thing. Therefore, to live, the relationship must be sustained and strengthened constantly. Love is like a plant. Without nurture and constant, careful cultivation it withers and dies.

We have found that anything in life which is worthwhile dare not be left to chance. A worthwhile relationship involves hard and constant work.

This is not an effort to produce some formula or suggest steps for a happy and workable marriage. We believe we have found certain ingredients which have helped in our marriage. When we have not added them in proper proportion our relationship suffers. Also, we have found that at different periods of our marriage one ingredient needed enlargement while another ingredient seemed less significant in adding flavor and balance to life. The following ingredients, however, are always needed for our marriage to be alive.

Commitment

Basic to our marriage is the kind of commitment we

made to each other before God and witnesses. This commitment is a great wall of strength during the attacks of discouragement, difficulty, and doubts.

All marriages experience difficult problems. This is normal. But commitment helps pull us through times of temptation, tension, and trial. One writer suggests that one of the reasons we make our vows of fidelity and love before God in the presence of other persons is that all of us know there will be times in marriage when it will be difficult to continue. We will be inclined to dodge our problems or to say it is no use. But we have pledged our troth and that in itself can be a help.

Betty and I committed ourselves to fidelity and to the permanence of marriage, with no thought of divorce as an option in case difficulty arose. Here too, the basic attitude toward marriage itself is most significant.

We committed ourselves to love, not only when we feel like it, but for better, for worse, when things go well and when things go bad. Love is an attitude which does what love requires, even without positive feelings at times. A couple or family which does loving things only when under the spell of a wonderful feeling of love will not do much loving. A mother gets up in the middle of the night to feed a crying baby, not because it feels so good to get up at 2:00 a.m., but because she loves. Betty and I have found that when we are committed to love, and do what love should do, our love grows and the feelings of love for each other flow.

We find it a help to make a commitment to communicate. Communication is the key to a happy marriage and its lack is the key to an unhappy one. When our relationship deteriorates, invariably it begins with an inability or unwillingness to talk about what matters and needs to be discussed. Even as we learned to know each other before marriage by talking, sharing, and discussing, we grow together now by communication. If communication is necessary for nurturing love in courtship, it is just as necessary for the maturing of love in marriage.

We find we need a commitment of time together. It is too easy in the closeness of marriage to go our own ways and pass like ships in the night. Before marriage we planned time together to do special things and go special places. We scheduled time just to be together, alone. We found that soon after marriage we started to go about our work with little time for togetherness. Time is not available unless we plan for it. But we must have time together if marriage is to work. As we take time daily, and sometimes even a day or two away alone, we learn to know each other in fresh and fulfilling ways.

We do face difficulties and differences. But because of our basic commitment of fidelity to each other for life, we have solid ground to work on. When we demonstrate love, even when feelings of love are low, we sense true love is present. And when we reveal ourselves more fully, we grow in love. Upon this commitment we have built our marriage.

Unselfish Living

We find that the more we forget our own rights and demands and seek the good of the other, the happier we are. Marriage cannot grow without unselfish giving and living. To think of marriage as a fifty-fifty proposition is not enough. That is a stance which seeks to protect self rather than to do everything possible for the good of the other.

Since most of marriage is the daily round of responsibilities and the common concerns of making a living and rearing a family, the way to happiness is to invest the common tasks with a quality which makes them lovely and happy. We find that most of us can manage enough muscle for the major things of life but that happiness results in seeking to be faithful in the little things.

Unselfish living means that we think of the other first, for it is still in giving that we receive. In enriching the other, we find enrichment. When we unselfishly serve each other, we grow in stature, satisfaction, and self-fulfillment. But when we stop giving and living unselfishly, affection dries up and resentment results. When we become too concerned for self, we react, strike out, and relationships deteriorate.

When we love each other, we make each other lovely; when we honor each other, we make each other honorable; and when we respect each other, we make each other respectable. Upon this kind of unselfish living and giving Betty and I have tried to build our marriage.

Mutual Openness

We find that the freer we are to share with each other who we are and how we feel and think, the closer we are drawn together. If as one writer says, "love can only grow by fuller revelation," then the degree to which we share thoughts and feelings represents the degree, depth, and quality that we are able to achieve in our relationship.

In a world where we are often driven to hedge ourselves about with defenses and pretenses, it is reassuring to be known fully and completely by another and still be loved. It is healing to share guilty fears, idle fancies, and hidden shames and still to sense acceptance and love. We can stand the battering of what the world says and does from the outside when we know we are loved and understood and accepted fully by one other person. We can continue to believe in ourselves if we who know each other best continue to believe in each other.

Openness builds trust which is basic to a happy marriage. Without trust a relationship soon disintegrates and is destroyed. But mutual trust grows out of frank and courageous sharing of thoughts and feelings—an openness and honesty with each other which lives in the light and avoids the disquieting doubts which grow in the shadows. As soon as we hide things from each other, we weaken the basic oneness of marital life. When we exercise openness and honesty, marriage becomes a wonderful adventure of healing, help, and happiness. We agree with the observation that joys are doubled and sorrows are halved when they are shared in the closeness of our relationships.

There is, however, a privacy which Betty and I have also practiced. It is a privacy which does not open the other's mail, does not listen to the other's telephone conversation, and does not examine the contents of the other's pocketbook. Marriage needs this kind of privacy which also builds trust and respect. We find that when we are most open with each other, love grows and life glows. When we are most honest in expressing love, what we feel, and what we think, our marriage matures. And when we share deeply, our spirits are refreshed and prepared to meet the problems of life. Upon this openness we have tried to build our marriage.

Mutual Understanding

We find that our marriage is meaningful also to the extent we seek to understand each other. Early in our marriage we learned that it is possible to live side by side, in the same house, and still be strangers to what the other is thinking and feeling.

This means that each partner should work hard to understand the particular needs of the other. We are not the same. In fact most spouses are very different in many areas. That is why we choose and need each other. One makes up for what the other lacks. Because of different backgrounds and experiences, as well as the fact that we are male and female, we must learn to understand each other if we are to be happy.

Further, this means we need to listen with the third ear and hear what we are really saying in our words and responses. Betty and I find that our deep desires are often hidden behind our surface feelings and reactions. Unless we really learn what is expressed by our reactions, actions, and feelings, we do not understand each other. It takes trust to tell each other exactly what we feel and need.

And when we do understand each other at one point or another we find that we can grow by making agreements. For example, early in our marriage a salesman came to the door. What he had to sell was attractive. We had little money and the item was rather costly. Each of us thought the other wanted the object and so we signed to buy it. After the salesman left, we soon found out that neither of us really wanted it. We agreed that in the future we would not purchase any item costing over fifty dollars which we had questions about unless we discussed it together first. This has saved us from many misunderstandings and financial difficulties.

When we try to understand each other, we feel appreciated. When we think of the needs of the other above our own, we feel fulfilled. When we agree on the small as well as the larger things in our relationship, we feel a sense of comradeship and partnership. Upon this kind of mutual understanding we have tried to build our marriage.

A Spiritual Base

Betty and I find that the closer we are to God, the closer we are to each other. George McDonald wrote his wife nearly a century ago, "My dearest, when I love God more, I love you the way you ought to be loved." In seeking to please God we feel constrained to please each other. As our commitment to God deepens, so does our commitment to each other. As we are honest before God we grow in honesty, openness, and love to each other. And the love we experience becomes more and more an expression of God's love for us. We picture our relationship as a triangle, with God at the top. The closer we come to him the closer we are drawn to each other.

Also healing of hurts takes place when we kneel together before God in prayer. We feel ready to meet the demands of the day when we rise from prayer. Our words are more precious to each other as God's Word is precious in our thinking. Our work and service take on meaning as we see it in the light of God's will for our lives.

If we are to have a spiritual base, we must be committed and give allegiance to God and to a purpose outside and beyond ourselves. We find that two people who live exclusively for each other will not grow in love. Merely gazing into each other's eyes and living only for each other will, ultimately, generate boredom, restlessness, and dissatisfaction. So we need a sense of shared destiny, a uniting together in a cause greater than ourselves. And God gives that as we serve each other.

Happiness in marriage, as well as in other areas, grows

deep and binding when it is not life's first object. "Pursuit of happiness" is a self-defeating activity. Commitment, joy, and happiness come not in seeking them, but when we lose ourselves in sharing them.

To make marriage work we need God. Day by day we recognize his blessing in our lives. Under his guidance, we receive the light we need to walk the path ahead. We live in the glorious assurance that he who planned our home here will not leave us homeless in the hereafter.

When we recognize God in the daily duties of life, we recognize each other as blessings from him. When we kneel in prayer we rise better prepared for life. When we give ourselves together in the cause of Christ's kingdom, we find our lives growing in greater oneness. Upon this spiritual foundation Betty and I have sought to build our marriage.

These ingredients are important ones in our marriage. They add flavor and firmness to our life together. They make our relationship alive.

The Spiritual Foundations of Marital Success

Paul Tournier

"We became one another's confessors and from then on we knew, as nearly as is possible in this world, each other's most intimate concerns."

Born in Geneva May 12, 1898, Paul studied medicine in Geneva and served his internship in Paris. In 1928 he took up a general practice and specialized in internal medicine in Geneva. His writings have been of inspiration to many in at least nineteen languages.

THE SPIRITUAL FOUNDATIONS OF MARITAL SUCCESS
Paul Tournier

We were betrothed in 1920, but it wasn't until 1923 that Nelly and I announced our engagement. We were married in 1924. At that time, in our society it was neither acceptable to have sexual relations before marriage nor to be married before having terminated one's formal studies. Morals have changed considerably, but I am not sure that young people in general are happier than we were.

Nelly and I were from the same milieu and our families knew each other. Her grandmother even studied the catechism under my father's instruction and both of us received our religious instruction from the same pastor, my father's successor at the cathedral. We struck up a friendship while we were both in his catechism class.

To be sure, we wanted to build a Christian home which meant that besides my evening prayer, we would from time to time have devotions. Since Nelly was timid, it was once more I who would read a biblical passage. I was educated enough to add a short commentary and a prayer. In reality, I was playing pastor and she was the well-behaved layman who listened to the pastor. However, enthusiasm for what we were doing was lacking. We both felt so awkward with it that we were hesitant to repeat this kind of a ceremony which was but a duty.

Otherwise we got along well. Neither of us had any doubts about our mutual love. Nelly flattered me with her unlimited admiration. She hardly ever ventured to contradict or criticize me, except on rare occasions when she would explode unexpectedly, which I attributed to her high-strung nature. I blamed her irritability on the fact that she had been seriously underestimated in her childhood. She was continuously compared with an older sister, who contrary to Nelly, had excellent report cards, and who adapted better than she to the regimented lifestyle of her family.

So I explained all that to her. I encouraged her to be more self-confident. But without realizing it, the more I lectured her and exhorted her the more inferior I made her feel. The same thing happened as I forced myself to keep calm during her outbursts, which made me proud of myself until I would flare up! Then both of us would cry and we would make up as a Christian couple should do.

Of course, this was rare and we were quite satisfied with our successful marriage, but our unsolved problem was ever with us. Then one day I was talking to an English colleague about another doctor friend. I told him that I felt sorry for my friend because his wife was high-strung. Then my colleague asked me, "Don't you think that if a doctor's wife is high-strung, it's her husband's fault?" I didn't say a word, but I thought it over. Was Nelly's tendency to be high-strung related only to her childhood, or also to her present circumstances? But I didn't consider myself in any way responsible for her temperament.

It was about that time that we were initiated to silent meditation in God's presence. That was in 1932. One evening in November at a friend's house I met several people who had recently been won over to a religious movement called the Oxford Group, because it was started by students of that university. I knew nothing about it except that it had been instrumental in morally transforming one of my patients with a bad temper. At the meeting were three well-known people from Zurich and several from Geneva, one of whom was a Dutch high official from the Society of Nations.

I was not very receptive to them, because I wanted to talk to them about their principles and methods, while they persisted in telling about personal experiences. However, the Dutchman said that for several months he put aside a block of time each morning, on the average one hour, to be silent and listen to God. Now that spoke to me, because I was well aware of my personal spiritual poverty in spite of my heavy involvement in church affairs.

So the next morning I rose one hour earlier than usual, without making noise, so I wouldn't draw Nelly's attention to what I was doing. I went to my office where I said to myself, "I want to see what difference it makes to listen to God for one hour." But the hour went by without anything taking place that was worth noting. I was able mentally to sketch sermons, but I had understood that it would be completely different, something much more personal. However, while leaving my office this thought came to me, "Once is not enough; I must continue." Immediately, this thought followed, "Well! This is probably a call from God."

I didn't doubt that the God of the Bible is one who

speaks because that is plain from the first page on. And not only does he speak to a people in a general way by dictating his law on Mount Sinai, but by communicating in a very personal way when he sends Moses to Pharaoh, when he wakes little Samuel, or when he commands Jeremiah to go to the potter. I understood that it was I who didn't know how to listen. So I continued my morning quiet time. Little by little I learned to listen—but not without frequent mistakes, of course. It is not easy to know if a thought is from God. But the essential goal is not to avoid all mistakes but to draw closer to God in order to listen better.

Two weeks later Nelly and I went to Lyon. We left early, had completed our shopping, and were having lunch. A bit apprehensive, I told Nelly, "I'd like to get back early, because I'd like to do something that I didn't get around to this morning."

"Oh, so would I," she said. "I got into the habit of meditating every morning like the wife of your new Dutch friend suggested."

We had a good laugh when we discovered that we had been hiding from each other the experiments we were both involved in. Of course, we were waiting for results before talking about it.

We returned from Lyon to try meditating together. But we discovered the same uneasy feelings we used to have during our devotions! I did not find inner tranquillity. Emotions spoiled everything and I didn't gain any thoughts at all to enter in my notebook. Fortunately, Nelly told me, "We need to start over again tomorrow and ask God to show us why we are so uneasy."

The next morning, I was already more at ease, but I don't remember what I wrote down. On the other hand, I never forgot what Nelly wrote: "You see, you are my professor, you are my doctor, my psychologist, even my pastor, but you are not my husband."

This was not a comment on our sex life. In this respect I was very much her husband. She felt a need for equality. Without equality there is no true communion, and outside of God there is no true equality. I am not thinking of equal ability but of equality as a human being, as a person. That is where equality comes in, different though you may be one from the other. I was an intellectual; Nelly wasn't. I was an arguer, an idea person. And suddenly, with one stroke under the inspiration of God, Nelly put her finger on my problem of which I was unaware. It took me months to gain an understanding of it, and years to grasp its full meaning, so sure of themselves are men with their rational ways as compared with the intuitive approach of women. In my loneliness as an orphan I had rejected my affective nature. To compensate, I disproportionately developed my intellect. I tried to make my way in society by manipulating ideas, arguments, and actions, all because of an inability to express my feelings.

Even my religion consisted of *ideas* about God, about Jesus, about mankind and salvation, about dogmas. And to my wife I would give speeches, lessons on psychology, on philosophy, on anything in the books. But my feelings, anxieties, and despair I was unable to express. All these emotions surfaced during our long periods of silence: painful images of memories, unconfessed guilt feelings, resolutions that were never kept. It was there that I, for the first time in my life, mourned the death of my father and mother.

Ah! How those first years of silent meditation together

as a couple transformed our relationship! I also learned how to genuinely listen to my wife. We became one another's confessors and from then on we knew, as nearly as is possible in this world, each other's most intimate concerns. There we would tell each other many things that we would have never told each other in the hubbub of daily life. Even between closely united couples one unconsciously weighs what one says and does not say. With so many couples, even harmonious ones, there are many subjects which are never brought up—often in order to keep peace, to avoid conflict. But in this way problems are repressed rather than solved.

The analogy with psychoanalysis is obvious, since Freud rediscovered in a secular way the power of silence and listening. But there are essential differences. Psychoanalysts remain silent, at least they don't say anything about themselves, while in meditation there is reciprocity and an intense quest for the presence of God. It is in God's love that one is free to verbalize freely. It is also the love of the psychoanalyst—a reflection of God's love, even if he doesn't know it—which helps a person say things he never dared to express before, and to burst the bubble of vanity.

So we have continued, at least once a week for more than forty years, these three-way meetings: God, Nelly, and I. This conjugal meditation complements personal meditation and vice versa. My whole career and my life's work followed as a result of it. This is what permitted Nelly to participate fully in my vocation without actually knowing anything about the problems of my patients. For in meditation it is my secrets that are involved, not those of others.

During an international session on holistic health

where all the participants knew us well, Dr. Paul Plattner used us to illustrate the doctrine of C. G. Jung on the evolutional function of marriage and of the social meeting of the sexes. Paul, he said, used to be a pseudointellectual who had repressed his already distressed sense of affecting while developing his objectivity. By getting in touch with Nelly he rediscovered his true nature, this sensitivity which made him the doctor you know about. Inversely, Nelly, who hadn't liked school, repressed the intellectual side of her and thus exaggerated her emotivity. By getting in touch with Paul, she learned to like working with ideas and succeeded very well.

It is not just a matter of discovering hidden marital problems, facing up to them, and solving them when possible. But each partner needs to grow, to go beyond self to attain that which C. J. Jung calls individuation. And finally, as the motivating force of the whole process, there needs to be a drawing near to God by the husband and wife who together have resolved to keep listening to him.

Marriage, a Lifelong Discovery

William E. and Lucy Hulme

"*Neither of us was ever resigned to a limping, inadequate, 'that's the way it is' marriage.*"

Lucy functions as co-conductor of clergy/spouse workshops, marital enrichment workshops, and workshops in Christian growth.

Bill has been a parish pastor, college chaplain, professor of pastoral counseling at Wartburg Seminary, a Lutheran tutor at Oxford University, and now is professor of pastoral counseling at Luther Northwestern Seminary.

MARRIAGE, A LIFELONG DISCOVERY
William E. and Lucy Hulme

For the past seven years we have been doing workshops together in which we use a tandem approach. We decided that since we each had specific concerns under the following topics that this approach would be fitting for this chapter. It provides the opportunity for us each to speak for ourselves. In discussing our marriage within this format Lucy (L.) will begin with her understanding of a positive element in our marriage and Bill (B.) will then present his. This tandem structure will continue through the chapter.

1. *Elements that Contributed to the Success of our Marriage*

L. When I think of factors in the success of our marriage, I think of *agreement upon goals and ideals.* While our different personalities and backgrounds demanded dialogue about the details of meeting these goals and ideals, our basic beliefs and assumptions are held in common. I could not have verbalized this at the beginning of our seeing each other as a serious choice of partner, but living our lives with Christ as guide and teacher was and is our goal. Through the years these ideals have been tested to the extreme, but I cannot see that the marriage would have survived our growth as individuals without agreement to the principles which drew us together.

B. We have experienced the importance of having *a good closure to each day*. It is important for lovemaking, for sleep, and even for how we feel when we get up in the morning. From the beginning of our marriage we have held evening devotions together. We depended on a successive discovery of challenging devotional books to keep this practice going. The time gap between these discoveries, together with the fatigue that comes at the end of a busy day, and the hope that the other will take the initiative, were hard on consistency. But we valued the devotional closure and decided on consistency, and on a method that would solve at least the initiative problem: each would take his or her turn on a day-by-day basis. We decided also to keep the closure simple. We focus mainly on prayer—for our children, ourselves, and our immediate concerns, and about the people we know and the times in which we live.

L. Our life has never been emotionally uneventful; so checking with each other at the end of the day seems natural. I tend to say "yes" to life and its opportunities, probably because of an innate *need to be creative*, which means I am as often following intuition as reason. One of the satisfactory aspects of our marriage has been the scratching of this itch. In this area Bill has been flexible and encouraging. In addition he has shared his own creative projects with me and allowed me to contribute to them. I work well as a team member and find it most fulfilling to be able to contribute to joint ventures. I have deep satisfaction in the area of creativity.

B. We both were fortunate to believe that our *sexual nature was God-given and good*. So we entered into marriage with good feelings about our sexuality. While I was initially bothered by the male pressure for performance, the security of our relationship helped me to work through this. Sexual attraction was and is a big factor in our relationship. We enjoy and look forward to our lovemaking, which in turn produces many good feelings that carry over into other aspects of our relationship. After 37 years it is as important and enjoyable as in our younger years—and probably even more.

2. *Basic Causes of Tension*
L. At the beginning of our conversations I may have seemed to indicate that my interest in sex is secondary. It is not. But before I could enter into a relationship which included sex, I had to have agreement upon what we as persons were about. Although there were and are unavoidable sexual tensions, a far larger cause of tension for me was an *unrealistic view of life. I found failure and imperfection hard to cope with*. Being a person who wished to be unlimited in experience, I put myself in line for some of both. Whether culturally, temperamentally, or otherwise caused, my response was depression. I had not incorporated failure into life.

Acknowledged or unacknowledged, existentialism in which freedom of choice equals responsibility became the dominant philosophy of my generation. Sowed upon the ground of Puritan perfectionism, it has produced some bitter fruit. Culturally a woman's worth was equated with her consumer power. The subtlest form was the homogeneous lifestyle depicted in advertising media of husband and children choreographed by the woman into a slick picture. A current survey shows church women still depressed about husband and children not meeting self-set standards which had their origin in advertising rather than Christianity.

While I now have some experience and guidelines for coping with this aspect of my life, it has left its mark. Culture says to not "have it all" at any given time is a judgment, and for this one bears responsibility. I had unrealistic ideas about the kind of world I lived in, and my own perfectability. I was depressed and found my changing moods hard to live with.

B. I am amazed at how caught up in my own interpretation of things I can get. Humility, I believe, is realizing how subjective and tenuous these interpretations of ours are. I judge Lucy according to these interpretations while assuming that hers are irrational. How could she think that? My empathy is solely with me. Since my empathy is not also with Lucy, the bridge it could build is missing. Rather than listening, in order to see things also from her inner world, I simply go through the motions. When we are so turned in on ourselves, there is not only tension but alienation. If Lucy responds in kind we have the painful task of working through to a more genuine reality.

L. For me, the tensions which lasted the longest and were the least resolved were the *in-law tensions*. Other tensions, even those caused by sex and money, were minor compared to this one. Obviously both families had some common ground. However, the carrying out of the day-to-day business of living was not similar. While large assumptions were the same, small ones were not. Large and small families, rural and city backgrounds, can account for some of the divergences. These failures to get along produced anger and depression in me.

Having married early with little work experience, and limited social experience of the kind which could produce adroitness in this area, I did not cope well. In addition, our living circumstances were vastly different from our parents, and we tended not to discuss any negative or problematic areas with them. I believe that parents of that generation were conditioned to be fulfilled by their children. I felt that I did not meet their expectations. If our generation had the same expectations, they were brought to a thud by the children of the 60s. I wish I would not have been so involved and threatened by these natural tensions and have reacted more wisely.

B. It is only as I look back, thanks to a sensitizing decade, that I see how caught up I was in *sexism regarding the roles of husbands and wives*. Being a clergy person only increased this sexism since clergy responsibilities encouraged certain assumptions. I assumed a tolerance on Lucy's part for any inconvenience I might cause her due to my work. On the other hand I thought I was being quite charitable if I stepped out of my own assumed roles and was helpful in ways that really were not incumbent upon me. Naturally when this happened I wanted to be appreciated. This was a source of tension hard to get at because it was obscured by these role assumptions. Our societal change has been helpful to me in hearing what was difficult to hear before.

3. *How Tensions Were Resolved*

L. It is not hard to see that both of us may be subject to our own interpretations, when you see that both of us have strong egos. Both of us had the assumption of equality in relationship and *neither of us were ever resigned to a limping inadequate "that's the way it is" marriage,* nor to a life of adjustment to smoldering resentment of manipulative cynicism about our marriage. We cannot seem to get on with things until issues are settled.

We were helped through recognition by the culture of our day that if high ideals and expectations of marriage were to be realized, communication skills had to be improved. I can see that this was an area of growth for both of us; the present "state of the art" of communication has been a great blessing to us. Our needs must have coincided with others. Wisely or unwisely, we have not sought marital counseling per se, but *new insights into communication have been very helpful to us.*

B. I brought into our marriage a big obstacle to communication, namely, *the silent treatment.* I had used it in my own family and evidently it must have paid off since I had become habituated to it. Even when I realized how obstructive it was to reconciliation and how much time and energy it wasted, I rationalized that it took time for me to recover from the wounds of a quarrel. Even when I would curb the overt manifestations of aggressive silence and manifest only the covert symptoms of emotional flatness or restrained initiative, I had simply moved from the sin of commission to the sin of ommission.

I finally realized that the silent treatment (or pouting) is a way of retaliation—of punishing those who hurt my feelings. Things changed when *I decided that this reac-*

tion to conflict was destructive and therefore had to end. Since God's reconciliation was always available, so reconciliation in our marriage was likewise available. To postpone a problem for a period of pouting was not only resisting God's Spirit but was ridiculous.

L. Your silent treatment was hard for me to cope with. I would often read into it incorrect data. I reacted to it with anger. *Anger is an old enemy of mine.* I have found it difficult to recognize and understand patterns held over from my family of origin. I was confused about my reactions to put-downs, frustrations, and manipulative people. This is one of the few places I recognize my interpretation of the Christian faith to have been harmful. In my need to be loving I obscured what was going on that was negative in my relationships.

In a family situation, I am explosive. I do not see this as helpful except to reach my true feelings and to help identify the real problem, which I have a need to resolve. When both of us work at our anger caused by the tensions of marriage, we do resolve it without resentment. Our reaching the point where *each brings to the other feelings which are bothersome has taken a long time.* I don't believe that either of us has a problem in sharing good feelings with the other; admitting and sharing the opposite took growth in trust.

4. *Counsel That Would Have Been Appreciated at the Beginning*

B. We had several traumatic conflicts during our three years of courtship which we eventually got over. We did not learn much from them because we did not know how to talk without resurrecting them. We did not realize that these were projections of what our marriage also would contain. If we could have discussed them, or better, role played them with a premarital counselor, it would have been an excellent source of help for our future.

A *personality inventory* would also have helped in this regard, but these were not as available then as they are now. When considered with a skilled counselor, the results of these inventories reflect our individual differences and the areas where these differences are potentially destructive rather than enriching. We needed this help to see more clearly who we were in our relationship and what putting us together into "one-flesh" would entail. We needed these inventories also to understand the models of marital relationship from which we had come and our tendency to assume certain things because of these models which we could not verbally state. We unconsciously identified with our parental models in emotional moments when our interpretative capacities were highly influenced by the past. Insight into these influences at the beginning would have helped us to know what was going on between us.

L. As I have indicated, I knew that I could have used some help, and I do not think that future events will eliminate that need. If older friends are any example, we can expect to need help later on and I hope then we can find the right sources. At the beginning of our marriage I would have been too defensive to ask for much help, but I would have been served very well if I could have understood and had the skill to use *the resources of frank and open discussion with friends*. I have always had supportive friends in neighborhoods, community service groups, and the church. I did not know how to ask for this help. I believe that for me this would have been the best kind.

For several years I have participated in the movement of support groups formed around a specific emphasis. Much stimulus for personal growth in secular and religious areas has come to me from this format. The nonauthorative approach with the emphasis upon finding one's own answer is comfortable for me. We ourselves have experienced the tragic death of a daughter. Among the many insights that I have sorted out from this experience are that physical, religious, and mental health, and a healthy marriage are real treasures. I feel that I have been fortunate in finding answers. I would say to every person, "Go find these treasures!"

5. *The Greatest Source of Help in Our Marriage*

B. I believe that the greatest source of help through the years has been *the practical effects of believing in God*. To us this belief means that God is for our marriage, that he was involved in our decision to marry, and that he will keep our marriage growing. We believed this, at least minimally, even when we were upset over the other's or our own behavior. Because God *is* for us, it seems that even these setbacks were within his redemptive providence.

In the later years of our marriage we have taken part in several *marriage workshops* which have been most helpful. Through these we have had the needed support to break through our knee-jerk defensiveness in sensitive areas and have discovered a new meaning to freedom—the freedom to turn off old tapes and to cut new ones.

L. The greatest source of help in our marriage has been our *commitment* to it. There have been times when my depression has overcome my good sense, when I have taken all responsibility for all outcomes of situations whose factors would require the mind of God to sort out. I then so easily forget the grace that daily has sustained me and mine. Bill's and my life has followed the cultural pattern. When we married, it was the husband/breadwinner, wife/homemaker pattern. It has changed to one of two careers.

I think that this change took place more smoothly than retirement may. Both of us are blessed with work offering satisfaction. I think we are aware of a subtle change in dependency. Things that at one time kept our marriage together are removed and we are now back to "love and commitment" to keep us together. Our faith in God has been tested to the extreme by tragedy, our marriage by the battles of fortune and living.

Through marriage we have participated in the final frontier of mystery. It has taken all of our resources. I feel fortunate to have survived. It has been a privilege. We were lucky to have found each other.

Commitment, Communication, and Creativity

David and Vera Mace

"What made a dramatic difference to us was when we came to understand the positive function of anger in a close relationship."

The Mace's founded the National Marriage Guidance Council. Later they developed the American Association for Marriage and Family Therapy and the Association of Couples for Marriage Enrichment.

COMMITMENT, COMMUNICATION, AND CREATIVITY

David and Vera Mace

It was Friday the thirteenth, and we consider it to have been the most fortunate day of our lives! We met in Scotland, and David's first words to Vera were, "What about it?"

It wasn't love at first sight, though. We became very good friends, and love grew out of our friendship. Our wedding was just four years after that first meeting. Both of us were Methodists at the time (we are now Quakers), and our common Christian faith was a basic element in our decision to marry.

The wedding took place in London. To the assembled guests, we declared that for us marriage was a vocation—we believed we could fulfill God's purpose for us better in a shared life than we could separately.

Despite our strong faith, we found the task of marital adjustment difficult. We tried to be open with each other, but our communication skills were poor and we often struggled with misunderstandings. We dealt poorly with our inevitable conflicts, and suffered periods of estrangement. We had trouble with sexual adjustment, and we managed our anger poorly. However, our conviction that we were meant for each other never wavered, and we now realize that our difficulties simply reflected how poorly equipped we were for adjusting to a close relationship. We sought help, but those to whom we turned were not better informed than we were. All they could offer was a few pious platitudes.

In due course our two daughters were born, spaced three years apart. They gave us great joy, and despite our interpersonal difficulties, those early years of marriage brought us some happy experiences. It is only in contrast with the much better understanding we achieved later that those early years now seem so frustrating. And it is because we believe most couples are no better equipped than we were that we have devoted our lives to attempting to provide better services to married couples.

Years of Enforced Separation

We were living in London when Hitler plunged Europe into war. As his armies advanced, England seemed doomed. Kind American friends offered a safe home to our children. We decided that Vera should take them across the Atlantic and then return. They sailed in June 1940, and their convoy got through with the loss of one ship. David stayed on in London and served as an air raid warden during the bombing.

The submarine war intensified, and Vera couldn't obtain permission to return. So, for three long years, we were totally separated. Even when Vera returned, she couldn't bring the children, who were separated from us for another two years. Six years passed until at last we were all back together as a family, in our own home.

After this harrowing experience, we made a deep commitment to rebuilding our family life, which from that time we gave top priority. We ourselves were already at work developing Britain's marriage counseling services. As a result of helping hundreds of couples, we learned what a complex and difficult relationship marriage is. In the seven years during which we built up a network of marriage guidance centers across the country, we gained for ourselves quite as much as we were able to give to others.

In 1949, the British government took over our organization, and we responded to an invitation to come to the U.S.A., where we have lived ever since. In 1960 we again responded to a call to develop a comprehensive service of marriage counseling in this country. During another seven years, we nurtured in the basement of our New Jersey home what has now become the American Association for Marriage and Family Therapy, with ten thousand clinical members. And again, we applied in our own shared life what we were continually learning about the marriage relationship.

As the years passed, we continued to learn more and more about marriage. It became clear to us that what we ourselves had lacked, and what most other couples lacked, was what Nelson Foote called "interpersonal competence." We saw that success in marriage depended largely on whether couples had, or did not have, what we called an effective "coping system." From our own struggles, we saw this as involving what we called the "three essentials."

What We Have Learned

The first essential for a good marriage is *commitment to ongoing growth and change*. Our commitment to each other was never in question. But no one explained to us that the choice "for better or for worse" is not a matter of fate, but is squarely in our hands. Going into marriage is like going into a career—we, and we only, are responsible for making a success of it.

The second essential is to have *an effective communication system.* Willingness to work at our marriage is not enough. We must know what to work at, and how. And unless we are fully open to each other's thoughts and feelings, hopes and fears, we can't clearly know what to work at, and the thrust of our efforts may be misplaced and wasted. We had a great deal to learn about couple communication.

The third essential is to *learn how to use conflict creatively.* We began by seeing conflict as something bad, and avoiding it. Then we shifted to the view that we had to endure it with fortitude. It came as a revelation to us to learn that conflicts in marriage are really "growth points," to be used as opportunities to deepen our understanding of ourselves and of each other, and to change for the better.

What made a dramatic difference to us was when we came to understand the positive function of *anger* in a close relationship. We had begun with the conventional view that anger is sinful, or at least an undesirable emotion. When we found that anger is in fact the defense system of the inner self, and that only love and anger working harmoniously together can keep a marriage in healthy balance—that was a vital turning point in our relationship.

Learning these vital lessons has meant a great deal to us. But putting them into practice was a difficult task that required years of effort, with many backward slides and many fresh starts. Because we saw that the rewards of sustained effort were tremendous, we kept at it. We still find it necessary to have a regular daily sharing time to keep in vital touch with each other. We make it a firm practice to clear up every issue that disturbs our relationship. "Nothing on the back burner" is now our motto!

We saw more and more clearly how complicated all this is, and realized that all around us couples were struggling and suffering as we had done. We began to reach out to others, sharing our own experience and learning, and offering help and support. This led to our early involvement, in 1962, in what is now the Marriage Enrichment Movement, and to our action in 1972 in establishing the Association of Couples for Marriage Enrichment (ACME). Since then we have been totally involved, in the U.S.A. and in other countries, in spreading the good news which has meant so much to us—through leading retreats for couples, organizing support systems, and writing books and articles.

We are now optimistic about the future of marriage. We see ourselves as an average married couple, just like millions of others, who wanted a deep, warm, close relationship, and worked hard to achieve it. At first, we seemed unable to reach our goal, because we just didn't know how. Then light and understanding came to us.

After fifty years of married life, we are closer and happier than we have ever been, and still learning and growing. What has been possible for us, we believe, is equally possible for others.

Making a Good Marriage Better

A. Don and Martha Augsburger

"Good marriages don't just happen. They may be created in heaven, but must be refined on earth."

As professor of "Work of the Church" at Eastern Mennonite Seminary, Harrisonburg, Virginia, Don has both taught and functioned as a counselor in the field of marital relationships.

Martha has taught and counseled many elementary school children coming from troubled homes.

MAKING A GOOD MARRIAGE BETTER
A. Don and Martha Augsburger

Not everyone can have the privilege of being married in Paradise, but that was the experience of Martha and me. She was from the Paradise, Pennsylvania, area and I from Western Ohio. We met in college. Our relationship emerged in our sophomore year after viewing each other from a distance that first year.

Our relationship was punctuated with prayer, both personally and in times of togetherness. Dating on a college campus can be both a good experience and at times frustrating. Much association and exchange are possible, although couched in the context of abnormal circumstances.

Martha graduated and began her teaching career after two years of college. I continued on and later taught in her home community. We married after my first year of teaching.

A successful marriage doesn't just happen. It is the result of continual evaluation and redirection. Martha and I have never taken our relationship for granted.

We have learned that *freedom to be and to become* has a unique influence on the improvement of relationships.

Having pastored in a number of situations, we have found that well-meaning persons have a subtle way of laying guilt trips on both a pastor and his spouse. Not only parishioners, but church institutions both explicitly and implicitly can become involved in placing controls on one's life. It took many years for us to come to the point of exercising enough freedom to enhance the process of becoming our authentic selves and yet respect those who placed demands upon us.

We are fully aware that guilt-inducing situations can emerge in many social relationships. However, the final decision to buy into that guilt experience is a very personal matter. We found that to grow in our relationship we had to work at freeing ourselves from reflecting the convictions of other people and crystallize our own. We have desired to become free in Christ and grow into who we are meant to be.

True freedom, we have found, is becoming free enough to choose one's own focus of commitment.

A second area of marital concern for us involves *communication*. Early in marriage communication was often blocked by selfish motivation or pure inability to bring a discussion to closure to the satisfaction of both of us. While one desired to push an issue to final conclusion the other might break off the discussion for reassessment and release of emotion or anger. Now we have learned that time to discuss and evaluate issues at the pace in which each is comfortable is of extreme importance. Each has a right to personal views, yet those views must be brought to the surface and evaluated for what they are.

Wholesome communication, we think, is the central core of deep commitment. For many years taking a trip together or going out to breakfast each Saturday morning, or a quiet evening meal alone has given us time away from children and other pressing duties. Communication needs appropriate environments and adequate stimulation to enhance wholesome relationships. We continue to work daily on this area of our marital relationship.

A third area of concern in our marriage involves *capitalizing on differences*. Persons who marry at a young age tend to choose a partner who is quite different in personality type. Those who marry a second time or at an older age are more concerned with matching personality types. Having married at twenty-two, we were intrigued by the differences in personal life and personality style. These differences have provided some homework for us both, making marriage much more than a boring existence of drab alikeness. If persons are matched in personality type, basically alike, life can be colorless. If spouses are different in most aspects of their personalities the possibility for trouble is greatly increased and a couple's homework is cut out for them. Finding ourselves alike in some respects and different in others has provided enough tension in the midst of commonality to make our marriage challenging.

No two people are completely alike in all aspects of personality. Each is a unique individual. Not even identical twins are identical in every aspect of personality.

It may be that when couples marry at a young age they tend to marry someone who is uniquely different because they do not yet possess the degree of maturity to accept someone like themselves.

Another view is that couples marry their opposites to complement their own personality or lifestyle. If this is the case, we need to ask, "Opposite in what respect?" Understanding the areas of alikeness and the areas of difference and working at helpful adjustments, we have found is a continually rewarding experience of growth.

A fourth area that helped our marriage along the road to success is our *understanding of covenant*. The vows taken at the marriage altar have been understood by both of us to be for life—not only for the length of our existence together but also for quality in relationships.

If marriages are to be successful, covenants must be taken seriously and become a guiding motivational force in daily relationships. Because of our covenant Martha and I consider ourselves to belong uniquely to God (the spiritual covenant) and to each other (the horizontal aspect of the same covenant).

The basis of lasting covenant is agape love. If this divine element is lacking, the marriage relationship may go limping into final defeat.

A marriage built on the erotic element only will experience a minimizing of the meaning of covenant as time goes on. The relationship of the physical (erotic) and the spiritual (agape) in the marriage contract, we have found, leads to enriched covenantal relationships.

Martha and I have found these four areas of continual challenge and of deepening impact on a marriage in process. We have not arrived at the ultimate in every aspect of interpersonal relationships, but we are working at it and that is what counts.

Summary and Proposed Direction

A. Don Augsburger

Persons can and do change, but slowly. Clear goals must be established in relation to what one wishes to achieve. Claim and build on every inch of progress made. Inches make miles.

SUMMARY AND PROPOSED DIRECTION
A. Don Augsburger

After reviewing the chapters by the contributors to this book and hearing the many helpful comments of thirty-seven couples I surveyed in a recent study, the following ideas stand out:

1. No couple is immune from the possibility of marital tension.

2. Good marriages don't just happen. They may be created in heaven but must be refined on earth.

3. Becoming aware early in marriage of possible difficult spots, and working cooperatively toward mutually agreed upon goals, can be the best approach for meeting potential hazards in marriage relationships.

4. Religious life and spiritual nurture have a positive impact on marriage.

5. A lifelong covenantal concept is of deep importance.

6. Most couples have adequate resources available to make marriage work.

Themes That Keep Popping Up
Poor communication patterns, selfish lifestyle, and lack of know-how for conflict resolution are three areas that

seem to be problematic in many marriages. The implications of these may be deep-seated compared with issues that are more surface oriented and subject to change factors.

Persons can change and do change, but slowly. Personality alteration can be painful. Lifestyles are built over a pattern of exposure in one's early years. To be able to change, or grow, a spouse must first recognize the deficiency.

Clear goals must be established in relation to what one wishes to achieve. The right tone of spiritual flexibility coupled with the assistance of resources, persons, or material, must then be encountered. Above all, don't become discouraged. Claim and build on every inch of progress made. Inches make miles. Thus one conquers.

Some Possible Solutions

Christian faith, lifelong covenant, and fidelity also appear to be basic factors leading toward successful marital relationships.

These areas all reflect a kind of preconditioning that happens in a wholesome experience in the family of origin. This is not to say that those persons who were less fortunate cannot achieve the same levels of success.

The challenge is for every couple to think in terms of their posterity. In providing carefully for the spiritual welfare of one's own family members, personality and lifestyle are positively influenced.

To practice "faith living" is contagious. To covenant to God and to each other in all the seriousness that heaven and earth can muster will have its positive effects. To practice hearing and to discover the thrill of being heard will make marriage come alive.

Who Can Help?

Many institutions in our social structure provide resources to work at the preventative side of family health. The church is one of these. Family tensions, separation, and divorce are evident both within and beyond the church. God's people are not immune. The church includes individuals who are trained in counseling, medical services, psychology, psychiatry, legal services, education, theology, and related fields. Some persons in these areas are deeply committed and are offering helpful service. The problems in marriage, however, still persist and are growing. The helping ministry cannot be left to the professional people alone. The total Christian community must take the task of family health more seriously. The congregation must become a resource for preventative services.

How can the church structure itself for preventative family ministry? We must first recognize the needs that exist in our congregations and communities. Some of the more obvious needs should receive immediate attention. Fellowship, nurture, and material needs usually are given top billing in a congregation. Less obvious needs are often pushed aside or not even recognized. When weak spots in family life are recognized, then preventative approaches can be taken which will help to avoid disaster.

The breakdown of wholesome communication should be a first area of concern. There are at least three types of families:

a. *The fused family* is caught up in one anothers' anxieties, both emotionally and psychologically. They can't hear what is going on in their own family setting.

b. *The chaotic family* is diversified in interest and direction. They miss each other in their communication attempts. One binding factor in their relationship is the fact that they occasionally live under the same roof.

c. *The open family* is one that is able to breathe psychologically and emotionally. They experience togetherness without threat and apartness without anxiety. In this type of family, parents can help their children become independent at the proper time and in a wholesome way, and children can assume responsibility creatively. In this type of atmosphere wholesome communication is much more likely. In fact it is difficult not to have good communication.

A second need is knowing how to give and receive love. Everyone needs to love and experience love and feel of worth to self and to others. Each person has an innate capacity to love and respond to love. This capacity must be filled with flesh and blood exposure. The person who has been given love finds it much easier to share love. Those who are not exposed to human love tend to reject God's love.

Cathy came to my office one day very angry. She said her father brought her to college and before they parted, he said, "Cathy, I want to tell you something. I love you." The reason she was so angry was because he had waited twenty-one years to tell her he loved her.

The ability to love meaningfully and to receive love wholesomely is a result of modeling. Persons must be loved for who they are, not for what they do. If this approach is taken, love takes on a qualitative rather than a quantitative dimension.

A third need involves the recognition of individual uniquenesses. All persons are born with great potential. Abilities must be recognized and developed into useful gifts. When abilities are not recognized and affirmed persons are inhibited in their usefulness. People must be treated alike, and differently. Individuality can be a tremendous asset to the family, church, and community if recognized, properly nurtured, and affirmed.

Most people find it difficult to affirm. They think it may cause pride. No one turns a deaf ear to honest affirmation. It is very encouraging yet humbling. Affirmation is much more helpful than ridicule. Honest affirmation is a strong incentive to spiritual growth.

A fourth need is to understand clearly the meaning of covenant. The master covenant is the result of a faith commitment to Jesus Christ. If this relationship is meaningful and the covenant aspect of Christian experience is taken seriously the marriage covenant will be less threatening. There seems to be a direct relationship between the ability to maintain a familial covenant and one's understanding of the meaning of the spiritual covenant. If a person is unable to submit to God through a life of faithful obedience, the marital covenant has a weak foundation.

Growing out of this primary covenant can emerge secondary covenants in areas such as commitment to personal growth, creative use of conflict, and unselfish and sacrificial lifestyle.

These four areas could be good beginning points for the fellowship of faith to exercise its concern in a preventative way.

The big question is "how?" It is a continued challenge to the church to help upgrade communication patterns. To model both graciously receiving and sharing love. To affirm one another in the midst of a growing spirit of competition, and to help persons understand covenant and take its implications far more seriously.

A congregation should isolate family problems, then structure settings to help meet such needs. When God's people free themselves from an attitude of condemnation toward marital problems, then couples will be more free to ask for assistance without embarrassment.

When preventative ministry is taken seriously, remedial services will be needed less. If the church does its task well the family will likely survive.